The Upstairs Country

The
Upstairs
Country

Alan Hill

Box 5 – 720 – 6th Street,
New Westminster, BC
V3C 3C5   CANADA

The Upstairs Country
Copyright © 2012 Alan Hill

Cover Painting: from painting by Candice James
Cover Design: Janet Kvammen
Layout: Candice James
Editing: Candice James

Library and Archives Canada Cataloguing in Publication

Hill, Alan - 1965

First Edition

978-0-9868097-9-8

silverbowpublishing@gmail.com
Silver Bow Publishing
ISBN 978-0-9868097-8-1

Silver Bow Publishing
Box 5 - 720 Sixth St.,
New Westminster, BC
V3L 3C5 CANADA
Email: silverbowpublishing@gmail.com

When the axe came into the woods, the trees all said,

'Well, at least the handle is one of us.'

Old Turkish Proverb

Acknowledgements

This book is dedicated to Frances, Thomas and Charlotte and my family in the UK, Canada and Australia.

I would like to thank Antigonish Review, Canadian Literature, CV2, Vancouver Review, SubTerrain, Mother Tongue Publishing and Silver Bow Publishing who have previously published some of the poems contained in this collection.

I would also like to thank Ken and Candice of Silver Bow Publishing without whose enthusiasm and support this project would not have been possible.

Last but not least I would like to thank my great friend Paul Bartholomew for his wonderful back cover write up and ongoing support.

- Alan Hill

Table of Contents

Visiting Malcolm Lowry
-Vancouver 1953

An unwilling Christ
that has been
slashed with an axe
by the pinheaded
pioneers
of provincial Canada.

His face is glowing
like a night raid on Dresden,
lit by the incendiaries
of sorcerers and demons,
tax payers, letter writers
and the non human eye.

He is squatting on a sanity
that has broken his legs,
bricked him deep in foliage
and ocean
at the back end
of the British Empire
under a sun
that has
lost the nerve to set.

He is fenced
in frontier space
in his driftwood Consulate for
the lost:

He is heir
to an impossible brief
that has been scripted
by devils.

He is a drinker
with a writing problem
being shamed

in front of a packed jury
of unfinished manuscripts;

Every day
is the day of the dead
for this mess of a man,
lipless and slivered
under a myopic thickness
of cheap glass,
scavenging for scraps
on the lip of a crater .

The Upstairs Country

Above us
in our postcard sized
spare room
our nanny has the Philippines

through Skype connected live
to her sons and mother

that she has
pixilated here, hot-wired
into our Canadian winter

her bus driver husband
just home from work,
bathing in the wallow
of his unfiltered cigarettes,
blows smoke
through our floorboards

tropical birds chirp

laughter

the wind
slugs slovenly
through the palm trees
into our stairwell.

Last Sunday a typhoon
shook the ceiling

sprinkled plaster
over Peter Mansbridge
as he read
the evening news

we heard the squeaking
of leaping furniture

as her whole family
sheltered
in panic
under the bed

the sound of a car
being hastily reversed
into a bedside cabinet

the crack of our
upstairs windows being shut
and blinds drawn

as the ocean flooded in.

Sleeping Furiously
i.m Pat Lowther

At Marine and Fraser
where you wrote your

'Intersection'

I am slapped by the
wind from your words,

the way they linger here
hunting me down

glinting, catching light

falling
stanza by stanza
from your stone diary
in to the
spurting headlights
of the boxy new buses.

The sun and moon
still linger here

the Lego apartment bloc
still stands.

It's salt now peppered.

Maybe in your time
this was luxury,
the voice of the new,
a pain lite future.

Now the only home to
cash free divorcees,
the indeterminate,

the unspoken poor,
the very ones
you would have spoken for
that I, that we,
do not

that poetry has failed .

There is that
phone booth
that you spoke of

that if I had the courage
I would walk into
beyond

to find you
pushing planets apart

seething with rage
at all this unnecessary loss.

In Mid Forties

On the morning
of my forty fifth birthday

I am a fugitive
from
the massacre of old age

hiding with wine
inside a garden

loitering
in the outer suburbs
of mortality

pressed

to the juvenile heart
of the spring growth

onto the beat
of the morning light
that is flapping itself
like a loose toupee
over a row of vegetables

in the hormonal blood
of the
freshly turned soil
that is ignoring me
in it's life giving
clumping and coupling.

A tooth for a tooth
an eye for an eye.

Yet it is beginning now,

this definable

encapsulated
sense of being
that
I never expected to know:

Starting in the middle

there is still time
for the repair
to outlive the damage.

Tweeting Lord Franklin

Spiking in a flow
of unsocial networking
the ice is stalking up the steps

crushing out the eyes of
pixilated sailors

scalloping the sodden wood
through the rifle pops of salt.

Canada is here,

clasping us on to the teat of winter

bellied beneath
the navigating drone of laptop

tiller and sail

the electroconvulsive
pressgang of milky tea

charting a book of faces
made mute in a
glittering dumbness

filling out the shape of a season
revealing its wing tips

easing under doors,
inflating under clubbing currents:

Terror and Erebus
herding in a glacial litter
of whispers

raising up the vapors
of the world wide nothing.

The History Lesson

Isambard Brunel
eases back after a heavy meal
and engineers
a zeppelin-sized cigar
out of the inside pocket
of his imperial waistcoat;

Queen Victoria
is entertaining Benjamin Disraeli
by juggling Indian diamonds
the size of Dodo eggs;

Just moments
before the invention
of the double entendre
Robert Stephenson
is polishing his Rocket;

Jack the Ripper
relaxes
with the Sunday papers

after a hard night's work;

Meanwhile
Under-Groomsman Hill
takes a break
from brushing
somebody else's horse
to slip a
lackluster glance
at the outstretched
fingers of his left hand:

It is of no surprise to him
that he appears
to be slowly disappearing.

Tasting Happiness

The steroid sized
windfall
from my father's yard
that I rolled to school
to eat at recess

that hung me
from the
muscled battery
of its
utopian knuckles

that whored itself
from the breaking jaws
of a spent snake

threw me
as willing sacrifice
under the razored pips
of a teacher's tongue.

Yet still I ate
through class,
through the day
the academic year

high school graduation

the
ritual under-achievements
of the workplace

through
sex and marriage
and divorce

my parents death
from

repetitive disappointment.

Bloody now
my teeth moved on
sucking
into the browning core

as I drove my truck
on a summer ride around
Stanley Park

preparing
my disguise
beneath
the deepening trampolines
of a rising heat

spitting seeds through
the open window
at unlucky pedestrians.

The Last Peasant

My family
had always been it,

Under-Groomsmen, Shepherd's Boys,
Day Laborers, the Shit Shovelers
thick-fingered Beast Killers

the resentful forelock tuggers
of a wasted millennium.

It was for them I tried to farm

wasted a day painting a barn

smashed fat rings into dilated snouts
of fear marinated pigs

fired the razored ordinance of bone
across the dumb stone yard

un-dammed an acreage of blood

a high pitched tillage
of feudal squealing
that emptied itself into a bottomless silo
of a December afternoon.

At 5pm
with the silence
of a launching torpedo boat,
I slipped my bicycle out of the yard
eased away.

The Season Ticket

At the Whitecaps
on game day one
the woman seated
next to me
anointed me Tony

It stayed that way

she convinced
and I too late
to ever tell her otherwise.

Then mid season
he was there
in occupation of my seat
feet up in a Nazi salute
drink mortared
immaculate.

Security
had me disappeared

I got arrested
for using his credit cards

attacked
for sleeping with his wife

made homeless
by my angry children
surprised
to be
living with a stranger

left in a foreign yard
kicking
a deflated soccer ball
against a wall.

Proclaiming a Republic

In the photograph
I am seventeen

a palace of youth
constructing itself in flesh.

I am beautiful, immodest,
throned at the
coronation end
of the dinner table

slim, brandishing cheekbones
you could slice peasants with.

A boy king,
emperor of a continent
of symmetrical features

my face a grid
of Versailles boulevards
towering over a pitiful slum
of the aged and less
genetically fortunate.

You would not recognize me now
after all these decades
of trying to hold it all
think it all, feel it all, control

ruling in my divine right
to cheap drink
and imperial over eating.

My ugly subjects
have broken through gates

pushed me
to the back of my tongue

slipped me in full regalia
into the bottomless democracy
of my own throat.

A guillotine of early evening light
is glittering
in the narrow valley
of the actual

is sharpening it's blade,
ready to splash cobbles
with blood and bile

proclaim government.

Coming to Terms

How I hover
like a slobbering jackal
at 'all you can eat',

run my eyes
up a woman's ankles
as if I was polishing pine

write poetry
as if I were a midget
playing tennis in the dark

close to the net
swinging wildly
knowing that
probability alone
will allow the occasional return

how I know that,
I am only in part, able,

that I am under the table
fishing crumbs
from greater men
through mean eyed cracks

that I am holding a banquet
of glittering smallness,
a oneness
of microscopic me-ness

I am host to a gathering
of lesser gods

a stalker
of the lustful promise,
of the inadvisably winking,
empty page.

Gardening the Dark

My obsessive wife
gardening alone
in the near night

being eaten alive
by her own maternity leave.

First she used
a cayenne pepper spray
then the soap and oil
then the A bomb drop,
the ladybugs.

Three hundred
premature things
let free
from a womb of paper bag
in their not quite yet redness
their sunless afterbirth

to eat
the already long defeated
aphids
squared in death
beneath the leaves
of the juvenile bean plants.

A birthing of bugs
spreading their wings
in a mother of all hungers
bleeding
under the loose jacket of dusk

that is spotting
white marks of starlight
through its torn pockets
on to the beetle hard back
of a summer evening.

The Cooking School

When you are quiet,
withdrawn from me,
it is then
that the worry starts

that you are in judgment

mixing my faults

beating my inadequacies

whisking
around your discovery
that I wouldn't eat
at any club
with me as a member.

Yet it is always the same,

the reassurance that you
are lost in food

composing that list
of your top ten deserts

the restaurant musts

a recipe for wild duck

the unpacking and repacking
of pasta sauces

the filleting
of the mental weight
of your new knife set

in admiration of
its ability

to cut through bones,
none of them mine.

Beyond you,
on the couch,
there are usually
our two children,
layered around each other,
grilling
under the rays
of a hot TV,

skin shimmering
like pudding,
ready to be served.

The Rented Piano

An angry zeppelin
of sound

a howitzer
of half hit notes
creeping greasily away
from tonality
with every finger punch
angrily defying every player

trapping fingers,
pushing away
the randy attentions
of the most ardent tuners

all those middle aged men
poshed up in
unfashionable leather jackets
and half mast pant legs.

It was my wife
it hated most of all

crumpled her career
as an imagined
concert pianist,
regurgitated her
benediction of 'Greensleeves'
burped up her Bach
had her in tears
leaving nothing
but the crumbs of songs

just childcare
and paying bills
standing between her
and a symphony
of mediocrity.

Suburban Warfare

Camouflaged in the yard
to avoid parenting,
thinking of running away
to another country,
returning
with a full head of hair.

By the runner beans
I spear my foot
on a bamboo stake.

An organic booby trap,

bane of the
amateur gardener
or jungle soldier,

blasting me backwards
into the rhubarb patch

into
an exclusive storefront
of my own blood

a flooding grocery
of DNA
laying out it wares
with bullet hole certainty .

Looking back to the house
I can hear my daughter
singing party songs:

maybe the hockey pokey
really is
what it all about?

The Art of Pruning

My aged aunt
has snipped me into twigs,
clipped me
into memories
too tiny to be seen,
seeded herself
though holes in time,
mulched history
composted the air.

Cousins, sisters, parents
fertilized and re-alive
dragging their new shoots
over my muddy rugs,
inviting themselves over
in unfashionable clothes
with their dated opinions,
embarrassing knowledge
of my bad habits,
bringing me down
with Victorian prayers,
annoying sing songs
around the piano
that I don't even have.

A great uncle
who disappeared
on the Somme
is sucking air from my lungs

performing the kiss of death
taking me in mouthfuls
spitting me
from a bedroom window
sharpening
the shovel of my voice,
slitting open the spring air
like a love letter.

Town Planning

From the drifting boat
she determined
to write
to her long dead parents
to her father at the front
in a war for which
she wasn't yet born.

She was young again
aged thirty
and living in Vancouver,
a City in which
she has never been
never will be in

out on the Fraser River
punching
against the spring tide
steering logs,
dead farm animals,
barn doors, clothing
and used plastic
towards the bank

in lone command
of the straining tiller.

Behind her
the steel and glass
of other people's futures
pimple upwards
against the horizon

Triffids of domesticity,
guardians
of the clean handed many
ignoring, preoccupied,
inching forward.

From the Inside Out

Her first time
kicking outwards
from liquid

airborne,
swiftly multiplying
expanding angrily
into the physical
binding herself
into the umbilical
of the real

her beauty
a cesarean
to birth and populate
a humanness
that she defines
yet can't yet be.

She is not yet
from this world,

a swapper of elements,
gouged out of a darkness

born
from nameless stones
and unvisited places

formed
from anonymity

begetting
land out of water

moving unseen oceans
into a broad un-traveled
continent of life.

In Daughter Time

So this is love
toothless
triple chinned,

a drooling deity
with eyes of spear sharp
Pacific sky.

A child
conjured from nothing
expanding her empire

rolling out
her blemish free blitzkrieg
posting me
to her distant frontier posts
her stockades in thin air.

I am her lost redcoat
in the wilderness
with my tri-corn hat
and loaded rattle
defending my baby queen,
my empress
of the imperial potty.

I am the crow
in frontier forests
hovering over her,
gone tame,
resting my claws
softly on her skin,
holding not scratching ,

guarding my fat chicklet,
so enamored
that I haven't noticed
she has already eaten me.

Birthday Girl

Your two years
laid side by side

glittering and alive
to the sense
that this is about you.

You are tensed
above your cake
with the fascination
of a baby tiger
eyeing its hapless prey,

not quite knowing
if you will eat or play
with its remains.

There it is,
that mathematic
exactness in your eyes

calculating on clues
spying
for ways to behave.

After the party,
driving home
we play peek a boo
with the moon

stalk it across
an empty highway,

flush it from brittle
October brush
over the tops of trees
that are alight
with a leafless

exuberance

crabbing their
tallest branches
into an
un childproofed
socket of stars:

Now it is my turn,
to watch you
for ways to behave.

Anglo- Asian

My newborn daughter

smacked into being
on the
blunt axe head
of the inarticulate

birthed
from a culture clash
that has slipped her
between us and away.

Airless and lipless
she has sounded
the imperial trumpet
of her own birth,

powered herself
in to being
from the
electrifying tonnage
of the earth

to be here suckling

latched on
to the dark
and slippery teat
of a Eurasian history
that is filling her up

that I cannot read
as it has yet to exist

that is loading her
with
its unsure weaponry

ill drawn maps

unknown beasts

hinted at
unseen wonders
from the edge of the world

as old,
powerless to help,
I wave
from an empty dock

watching her
as she emigrates.

Sleepers Awake

Around 1am

my son awakes

crow crying
from his crib
into
the void
of milk and nipple

then my daughter
tumbling on radar
down the stairs

thrashing
through her fright

Dinosaurs
one step behind

chalking out her profile
in whip crack breath

elevating her
on teeth of lightlessness
into our sheets

Later still
the cat jumps up
treading
the night's pale coins
in to my flesh.

Then there are five
in a queen size bed

our thoughts
sucking breast
digging claws,

throwing anchors
into the darkness

molding us
in silent radiance

curving us
in the
nighttime's crinkled ear

weaving us
into the
vine woven life flower
multiplied
in its shrinkage.

Insomnia New Westminster
(Population Unknown)

At 2am
an ant on the ceiling
with the proportions
of a medium-sized Rex Murphy

an eagle rotisseried
on a lattice
of faux wood window blinds

Arbutus trees, stripped naked,
teasing,
frigging their come hither leaves
against the frigid glass

a militia of grasshoppers
rustling their little legs
across the bed head
with an Ignatieff
of ineffectual rifle fire.

There are
musket laden woodsmen
under the eaves,
playing cards,
drunkenly sobbing
for the loss of centuries,
of families and land
in old
Dorset and Gloucestershire

hunters
laying glittering, jawed traps
spiked with the poisoned tears
of a forgotten Europe

spying
though knot holes in the walls

whispering insults
and calls of love
in a voice
that I can only recognize
as mine.

Older Brothers - France 1963

In this photograph
I am not born yet

My older brothers are
guarding my entrance

scouting out my future ground
in matching t-shirts and shorts

armed in mouths, eyes and hair
that they are holding for me.

Two boys of eight and ten
on a Mediterranean beach

in the certainty of an August heat
that pins their uncertain smiles
into a thicket of steady light

holds them there

jamming clock hands tight
denying time

if only just for them,
just for this moment.

This was before it all

schizophrenia, social workers
the police, the unwilling neighbors

the lives disemboweled
by apathy and accident

couriered away
to unknown destinations
under the ambivalent cosh

of those paid to care.

Whatever they have not been since
they were that day

giving me heat and light
a stretch of empty sand

the grains of it
that I am finding still
in socks and old pockets

in the grit of my breath
in the grip beneath my feet.

Without a Net

My St Christopher
before the fall

before his drinking

the barbed uncoiling
of his mind
into a picnic free for all
for cops, physiologists
spiteful neighbors
pitying strangers

before it all
there was the holiday.

Him carrying me
his little brother
on his shoulders
up a stretching vein
of mountain track

a delicate line
winding itself airborne
to hook within the gullet
of a hardening fog
to leave us eyeless
in a radar of faith
to leap from rock to rock.

I felt it
as he jumped us
into oblivion
the smack
on the base of his boots
as he found it

this time
only coming to his knees.

The Bewilderbeast

While playing at hide and seek
I left my wife and child

slipped into a gap
behind the hanging jackets
that nobody wears

that haunt their past uses
and done identities
like desert parked Boeings.

Knowing I could never be found
I stayed put

only slipping out at nights
to feed and prowl

nibble at cheese,
take slugs of milk,
leave giant droppings in the kitchen

rearrange the fridge magnets
into noncommittal messages
of love
abandon crumbs of myself
to be trodden into the carpets

drop whiskers as divining rods,
tracks of who I am

could have been

scattering a scent of hints
that one day
I may return.

Up On the Roof

He was one step away

hanging one leg
as a probe
over the lip of life

momentarily
latching his breath
on the rusty guttering
of the tenth floor rooftop.

A middle-aged man
splayed on an apex of slates,
slipping
in flat soled plastic shoes
on the thin skin
of the V-shaped roof.

He could feel the disgrace,
knots of it
bursting
in the back of his head

knowing
that he was
letting someone down,
although
he did not know who,
that he was
jumping the queue
between
this life and the next

that he owed it to someone
to show patience
to wait his turn.

Below him

he could see
the vast machinery
of automated life

Firefighters, cops,
the male fraternity
bonded
in the spreading of nets
the unstrapping of ladders
the unpacking of bullhorns
and blankets,
the strategic parking
of fat bodied trucks.

This little army
they have made of life,

these ambassadors of being

swarming with a certainty,

that just to spite them
made him want to live.

Astromine Domine

Every day at 8am
the aging ambulance
comes for him,
collapses
outside our house,
its engine a cut wind pipe.

My brother
as usual, ignores it -
leaves its insistently
horn hitting driver,
with the face
of an accidentally
washed bank note,
air locked behind glass.

He continues with the
unpeeling
of his layered head
over a late breakfast

laying out
his many sci-fi magazines
on to the curdling linoleum

his nebulous spread
of Star-Trek, Dr Who

that is launching him

allowing him
this space walk
on the hard star
of his own madness

just a driveway away
from a universe
of depthless disinterest.

Beating History

It was just after
Stalingrad, Hiroshima, Auschwitz

had goose-stepped around them
yet not touched

that they met
over clumsy feet
at a trade union dance

in the putting forward
of a mutual delegation
of poorly negotiated footwork.

Here
were my Father and Mother
in nineteen fifty one,
before the teenager existed,
dressed as hopeful applicants
to their older selves

he
in occupation of the haircut
and a version of the suit
he was to have
for over sixty years

was wearing
for his
diamond wedding speech

...as upon the podium,
with loosened tie

he waltzed them
with his words of love.

Après-Ski

They met
on Cypress Mountain
on the day of Pearl Harbor

drinking themselves into battle
in the ice boned lodge,
that they couldn't have imagined
would outlive them both.

As their eyes locked on
the torpedo planes were launched,

over their first words
the California was hit,

by the first drink
the Maryland went down,

by the time
he had his hand on her knee
the Arizona slipped under
leaving two thousand sailors
clinging to inflating love hearts.

launching bubbling bullets of heat
into a heavy flak
of a December snowfall,

a shrapnel of soft kisses
scattering bartenders
as customers forsook air,
lunged for weaponry
dodging the igniting pine splinters
as a magazine
of inflammatory cocktails
blew skywards
mushrooming the memory
of their first kiss against the sky.

The Viennese Waltz

They stole it all
And as an afterthought
They took his old LPs.

Brahms, Beethoven
Wagner and Strauss
sieved from a
fifth floor doorway
through the
utopia gorged fingers
of a Bavarian Sergeant

busily disowning his own

grown tainted
by the whoring
red lipped pouting
of a tempting Eden

flexing
his
thick skinned lebensraum

composing
the atonal spaces
where there had
once been music.

Secondhand Daylight

Grandma
never did get over what she'd been

the civil servant,
landowner in the Mekong Delta,
the family's' eyes and brain

now the somebody turned
Vancouver nobody

washing dishes, cleaning offices
collecting empty cans

shoplifting to fill the gap

batteries for electronics
that we don't have

chocolate for our guts
already multiplied to western size

newspapers
that we can't quite be bothered
to read

the family-sized tube of Anusol
that I plan to save for my retirement.

It's not all bad
she has it still

the rice paddies
thieved in hidden pockets
under Canada Way

The Pacific sunset
held out like a credit card

the respectful nod of the store detective

the verandas on East Hastings
from which to view
the water buffalo circle and descend
in to the fat cuffs of summer light

to find themselves detained
against the ocean's edge.

An Eventual Victory

Mapless
in the Parisian backstreets
we are brought unarmed
against the ambushing
brickwork of the university

where your grandfather studied
and then was studied
by the colonial French

who philosophized
to bleach him white,
reform the broken him
as almost trustworthy

un-yellowed, civilized,
Indo-Chinese not Vietnamese

suit him
in the shabby fabrics
at the roll end
of a low rent empire

sculpt him
into something far too good
for his own people

although not quite
good enough
that he would dodge
the Viet Cong bomb
that magicked him to meat
in a Saigon street.

Yet we are here
after fifty years

laying an easy claim

to his walkways

the daughter
of his bastard child
that he discarded
as low class garbage,

his grandchildren
that he never met

who are pitying
the silent students

scrubbed
skinless by their knowledge
behind
the metre thick brick

guillotined from the
liberty, fraternity, equality,

the un hurried manifestos
of the spring sunlight.

The Still Planet
i.m James Graham

The garbage bag

a broken hostage
of hospice leftovers

slumped
on the kitchen floor.

Mathematically
I unpack

the tube of toothpaste
that has
sprained and spent itself
over your tweed pajamas

the crumpled kill
of fake fur slippers

the half gone bar
of unscented soap
frozen in its
Matterhorns
of unclimbed cleanliness

the unfashionable watch
that still has
chips of your skin
speared
into its elasticated strap

that puffs on,
making a mockery
of the exactness of time

not knowing
it has already stopped.

The Trouser Press
i.m. Nicholas Alders

It was my uncle
that wove himself a life
out of the flesh stained fabric
of the Third Reich
sewed himself together
in the early hours
of bedsit dawns

forcing
his bloody fingers
to stuff back in
his broken Jewishness
in to
the twitching Frankenstein
of the new man
he was starting to become
caught between cultures
and languages,

hovering himself
over the wet winter rooftops
of an alien City

the landlord's Trouser Press
watching him
from the top of the stairs'
its steel jaw
a clamping fontanel
of banister and skylight

cocked and folded

hair triggered

like a waiting Panzer.

The Dust Up

For a while she lived to dust

beyond reason, unseen,
tap-dancing like Fred Astaire
over couches and cushions
held mutely
in their plastic straightjackets

sweeping behind knickknacks
with the precision
of a neurosurgeon

herding dirt, recalcitrant fluff
in to captivity
with a feather tipped springbok
of a domestic colonial cop

carving crucifixes
of acidic polish
in to browning flesh
of unworthy table tops.

When everything is dust
then the world will be hers

in her pinafore and gumboots
skipping across centuries
pole-vaulting planets
rearranging galaxies
within a frame of china cats
and John Constable place mats:

praying at a
mantelpiece of light,
laughing in the face
of a tidied Eden.

Strictly Personal
i,m Eddie Laird

The accident
smacked cracks
into his head
left him lying
on a country road
 improvising
under a winter moon
his Vespa
decomposing itself
across a stave
of empty highway.

It was after that
he tried to teach guitar
would often sit alone
in diminuendo
for students
that would never come
with only
Captain Beefheart
and his Magic Band
for company.

Zoot Horn Rollo
The Mascara Snake
Antennae Jimmy Semens
Rockette Morton
throwing notes
in to the orange claws
of summer light
quavers, crochets,
minutes floating up
for him to catch
squeeze between his hands
into a rarer sound
a coda
that could still be him.

The Last Armistice

Finally it never happened
as he had got the wrong man

In the Vancouver rush hour
he ambushed me
on the Cambie Street bridge.

Gavrilo Princip,
tucking his 100 year old beard
in to his gortex,
drove two bullets through my head.

Changing
into a higher gear of senility
he had mistaken my Honda Civic
for the Archduke Ferdinand's
open-topped sports car.

It was then
that the remaining splinters
of my grandfather's bones
began to slip through Flanders mud
and reconnect.

As he dragged his corpse
towards the coast
the muscle then the flesh
coagulated into shape.

Not long later he was back
to the first day of summer
in 1914,

just out of school
sitting in the sparse front room
of his fathers farm cottage

the blank pages

of an unread newspaper
lying cold under his fingers

his whole life
loading itself up before him

his untaxed forces
welling at the unmarked border
of his conquered boyhood

readying themselves to advance.

The Death of a Thunderbird

The table at the remembrance service
is crowned with a hockey stick,
hard as shotgun
as hair triggered as a swollen vein.

A ritual placement of samurai wood
a nesting physicality
framing its canopy
over the fading team shots
from the seventies.

Homegrown boys
graduated out of East Van lanes.

Sons of veterans,
pressed from modest soldiers' homes
with basements and yards

the occasional wide-bodied family car
with its skin bleeding
from obsessive polishing.

An Infantry of adolescent men
in sideburns and Afros

ill chosen knitwear
hormone curdled leather.

For the first time
the children of the working classes
in education, pulling out the shots.

Pioneers with no maps or experience.

We eulogize upon his monster hit,
where it took him,
over the goal, out of the stadium,
over the ocean, Stanley Park,

slashing across the City Center lights ,
slicing through a pinata of stars,
the nightclubs and the parties,
the drink, the drugs
in the washrooms
of the most exclusive bars:

It was in darkness
where he would find light

pressing his hands up

mouthing inaudible pleas
from beneath center ice.

After Ginsberg

I saw the best minds
of my generation
destroyed by Facebook.

Who were celibate in the
Ikea clip-together dawn,
striving, empirical , faking it
for the one-eyed shrew
of mortgage.

Who were
the uncommitted bored

dismembered by sinister editors

sentenced to unreality.

Who were wasting time
in coffee bars
in the pretence
of creating the future of the novel
while obsessively checking
their email.

Who were lost
in naked hysterical
homage to the web

giving their identities away
to governments, con men.

Who were mental mince meat
in the dying shopping mall
of the poorly lighted imagination.

Who tramped in bloody feet
from badly fitted Birkenstocks.

Who worshiped
at the bloated
Moloch Wal-Mart
of the perpetual new,
silver shiny petite.

Who solved the world
Its mysteries and agonies
through the purchasing
Of a hybrid car.

Who had Satori
from second life to third
in a sunflower sutra
of the absolute cynical
post modern heart.

Who were butchered
out of their own bodies
to last nearly a week.

The Hunting Party

We gathered the hounds

the cutlasses and shotguns

marched out
towards the heart of love.

It lay beneath us
tropic, sulfurous, deserted

although at night
we knew it left its lair

to feed on shepherd boys,
lost travelers on the moors
teenagers with acne
I.T. consultants
and the aging single

dropped itself from trees
on to the backs
of the married bored

on to those
who have espoused
their happiness
a little too loudly,
a little too vehemently.

We had no uniform or creed

some hunters
came in tweed
some in loin cloths,
others
in top hats or suits of armor.

Some arrived from cities,

men came
from other centuries,
past and present,
forming lines
and throwing nets.

Everyone of us knew that fear

that
it had changed its tactics

once again
was promising utopia

tormenting us
with eternity

then slipping away
uncaught
to wave a bloody arrow
at the sun.

The Magic Christian
for Paul Bartholomew

After kedgeree,

whatever that was,

a gang bang
of meaningful looks

she prayed him into bed.

Progressive Rock
early Genesis or Yes
played by a man
with no chin
on a guitar
with three necks

a cannonade
of oversize candles
dripping onto her
bedroom battlements

as she gave him Jesus spells
in hormone concocting
whispers

as with shaking hands
immaculately
made concrete
he manhandled
her petite feet

virginally shaking
walked on water

fished his fingers
up her legs
into a flow

of low rent hippy fabrics:

Twenty years on
he has that erection still

framed now
behind protective glass

bulging immaculate
beyond
a line of crucifixes,
a lasso of fresh garlic.

The Empty Backpack

On the bus
outside Brisbane
he kissed the Irish
woman girl
with the
touching eyebrows

saddled himself
to a Greyhound
that raced them away
in a benediction
of puckered lip

ringing them
in the slapping heat,
of repetitive movie features

the hellishly compulsive
Forrest Gump
that has been showing
since Darwin
a day and a half ago

that has turned them
on each other
in a
twinkling death sweat
of lust and despair

sucked them
deeper into the flesh
of the
flaming plastic seats

into a tropic tongued
exploration
of the tonsil rocked deserts,
the un-trekked interior

of the sexed.

He cannot stop

doesn't want his tongue
returned to him
when there
is nothing to say:

there is just
this empty moon
beyond the griddle glass
framing this antipodean
landscape
that
he can no longer read.

The Battle of Britain

At the dry heave
east London pub
where we stopped
for our break-up chat -
it was all old men
in crumpled suits
each sentence ending
with the click of pool balls.

Then the
unexpected entrance
of the podgy stripper

bar dust tipping out
its guts
to "Like a Virgin"

the red tassels
on her breasts
the swinging propellers
on a burning Lancaster

broken bean bag thighs
bulging from overuse

collecting her payment
in a dirty pint glass
handed around
by the clientele
like an unwanted
murder weapon

mapping out
a pathway
through
the winking slot machines
for my reluctant arousal
your insistent tears.

I Saw You
from the Georgia Straight

I, man with two eyes
you, woman with hair

we passed on the seawall
you smiled.

I, woman with scarf
You, man with nose

on the bus to Waterfront
you were holding a book.

Me, serving Pizza
You, parking your BMW
into the cleavage
of the sunlit lot .

I love you
you ignored me -
come for coffee.

You, Omnipotent
conjurer of light an air
casting runes of sushi roll,
spells
of frappuccino froth ,
seeing me all at once
and for always

call me sometime -
please.

On The Water's Edge
Cornwall 1973

The boy about my age

drowned

becoming matter

object connected
to the digesting surf

his loose limbs
yearling torso
swallowed
then re-birthed
on to the beach.

His father arrived
shaking like a
disintegrating planet

splitting in panic

only being held together
by his
unfeasibly tight
swimming shorts.

It was then
that it came to me

this jealousy
that has never left me

of seeing people
in love.

The Disappearance

Just some certainty

that is all she wanted.

Love and patience,
maybe a little of both at once,

with a lifetime ahead of them.

Two young people
with heavy sabers
of empty rhetoric

discovering the easy power
of bending and snapping.

He did not follow as
she walked away

too young to know a
beginning from an end

or that forty years on
he would love her still

that he would miss the
unborn children

the lost familiars

the imagined life they
never had.

Going, Gone

Burnaby pioneer homes
deflating in the
slackening rigor
of ancient zinc roofing,

slipping their arthritic timbers
into clumping landscape

homes slotting
ever more squatly
into the scuffed knuckles
of the shortening fields.

Broken tractors
rusting ploughs
that have been struck dumb
in the detritus
of their lost function.

Farmland
softening
in the annexing blandness
of an armed urbanity.

They don't mean to
but they do,
some of them are good men,
yet, inch by inch,
deal by deal,
little bits of something
get pieced together
into a bigger nothingness

and all that will remain
will be concrete and tires.

The New Recruits

Two teenage boys
swallowed whole
within the camouflage
of their oversized uniforms

singe file
under a detonation of rain,
sliding themselves
on a shrunken gum
of sidewalk
between highway
and marchland.

They are caught
in a light
that is liquefied
and leaping into the Pacific

air and water clasped
under a hardening city nipple
of knitting glass and steel
cribbing down, uncoiling,
into the inner nature
of a fathomless offshore.

Adolescents
caught in the open
on earth
negotiating a return to ocean
sinking itself beneath sea level
dissolving itself between car tires
in suspended animation
above a mirage of roadway
pale as eggs

an eel skin sky
turning itself inside-out
wriggling free

In Condominium We Trust

It is a siege fort of swan bone steel
and six pack muscle glass

that is throwing a wasps' nest
of skin tone shadow
across a line of pasty Cedars,

hardening itself
behind the barbeque cladding
of its buttressed battlements
that are sterile and glinting
with the disinterested sincerity
of well-scrubbed bedpans
or the sharpened instruments
of an overconfident surgeon.

A hijacked jet of living space
that has crashed itself
into the brain stem
of a million private places

a hermaphrodite of high rise
reproducing itself through
a telegraphic frottage
of wire and chrome

throwing out the shapes
of newborn speech

the words of new community

of sentences and slogans
not yet compiled

that have shot themselves alive
out of the mouths
of the battlefield artillery
of molded and unstable reasonings

out in to the
feeble wooden colonies
of the mind

out in to the new frontiers
of internal space

to pour their molten polymers
of neighborhood

guide their freshly pressed utopians

their plastic Peace Corps devotees

into a blindfold spacewalk
in to the napalm spitting
eye of an irritated something.

The Garden City

Two coyotes in a fission
of atomic toned teeth
poised on the perimeter
of a feeding frenzy
beyond the veal toned
gravel walkway

become a totality
of self possession

hunting and gathering
wired into a darkened square
of nature littered swampland
pinching themselves
between the fleshy gouges
of the surrounding highways

the encroaching strip mall
that is cracking its knuckles
over the bleaching condo tops.

Within the kill
a solitary whimper
crawls itself up the spine
of the fuel vapor
from an accelerating truck.

A galaxy of adolescent grass
flexes itself
to frame and hold away
the butting traffic
that is fidgeting in itself
like a junkie
in dead man's Reeboks

muttering other words
not known or said
afterthoughts like breath.

The Waiting Room

The three of us

the Zen Abbot
with his two new conscripts
with our Buddha sized eyes

tripping over
the candy canes of
karmic man traps

limbering around
the egoistic gunships
of our rising thoughts
mapping our way
through the star charts
of our adolescent acne
the wilderness
of our inadequate facial hair
into the small back room
of an East Van temple.

He almost whispers it
"sometimes I watch the tree out there
and for a while I have enlightenment".

The three of us turn
through the un-oiled gears
of the silence
to watch the scrawny maple
swaying like an angry pimp
in the back garden:

Not knowing what to say
to these other strangers
we all intently stare,

waiting for
something to happen.

The Bitter Withy

Slithering
from the bus
on Christmas Eve

pregnant with presents
- mainly for myself

I met
the young Jesus
playing soccer in the street
who offered me a game
-which I refused.

Giving me the finger
he escaped
over a bridge
he had bolted together
from the
beams of the sun

in angry pursuit
I slipped at mid span
showering my parcels
over the roofs
of condominiums.

Clutching on
by my fingertips.

l looked back
across Stanley Park
and prepared to drop

on to this City
whose very mainspring
is the haunting fear
that someone somewhere
may be happy.

The Historian

In old age
he had a condo
on a sandstone cliff top
that rattled
like ill-fitting dentures.

A retiree,
pushed out of history

only to turn

find it
chasing him down
the street

have it appear,
in combat gear
and ski mask
to crack open his front door

break china
and tear up paper.

Clutching his betting slips
and boiled sweets
he retreated
to the top
of his bunker sized TV.

Taking a steak knife
he sliced off his own head

placed it carefully
under his arm

crawled
inside his own mouth
and went to sleep.

On Wall Street

My tongue slid mid lick
from the butterball of creamy cash
to end up pinched between
the insistent teeth of a fat Texan.

I am French kissed
by the anonymous rich,
date raped by a man
that doesn't know my name
in a gentleman's club,
a Mexican brothel,
a glass cathedral.

The sun is low, lights have blown.

I am surrounded
by rapier lined young Caesars
oozing stallion smell, suited, imperial.

There is a bull, hooves crossed,
reclining on a bright red couch
and sucking on a soggy fleshed cigar.

A bear,
somewhat apathetically,
examining his claws
is slumping
over the half read business section
of the New York Times.

They are looking through me
as if I am already a ghost:

a movie plays,
there is a blur of disrobed bodies,
yet nobody is hard
the passion spent,
not even money lasts forever.

A Movie Review
-Melancholia

Some weddings
end in drunken scenes,
old partners
dealing tired passes,
the risqué revelations
of a best man speech,
upsettingly
persistent hangovers,
embarrassing uncles
making
inappropriate advances,
indigestion.

Some weddings end
in immeasurably large
fiery planets
incinerating the Earth,
immaculate blonde
newly weds
having alfresco sex
with fortunate strangers,
in a confetti of dead sparrows
tipping themselves
gleefully over the lawn,
a horse collapsing
in slow motion
on the veranda
of a medieval castle

a Rhinish super woman
bathing naked
in the Aryan blue light
of approaching death
her perfect breasts
a nesting of panzers
inciting surrender.

The Lotus Eaters

The dead tree
$\qquad$ on 2nd and 6th
with the clusters
of scar-red apples

strung up still alive
in a total alopecia
of leaflessness
between
the femurs
of brittle branches
that have twisted
into the black flesh
of constellations

each fruit
a hive
of rotting planets
hanging on a gibbet
of solar systems

snapped angles
of light
and weightlessness
endlessly expanding
possibilities.

A platoon
of middle-aged runners
head past at speed

ticking
to a metronome of fear
that is expelling itself
through flooding spandex,
accelerating against
the threat of an
expanding nothingness.

The Bagpiping Scientologist
Granville Street, Vancouver

A teenaged boy held hostage
within the inflating scurry
of his pumping cheeks,
kidnapped still alive
within his translucent skin
of uncooked egg

massaging the pipe bag
to his chest
with the clutching
of an apprentice strangler,
uncoiling a spiral jetty
of cobra spat notes
in a melodic incontinence.

He is hijacking
these prehistoric jigs ands reels,
unpicking the ritual lattice
of vibrating air
through which the rural poor
once conjured out walls
between dark and light,
earthly un reality, the unearthly real,
the pulsing propitiation
of rough shod pathways.

He is flinging
this priceless archaeology of sound,
melody by melody,
note by note
over the heads
of a dissonant symphony
of shoppers.

A not quite man
taking music,
crafting back into silence.

Transit Twilight

Mount Baker,
a constipated owl
squatting over the border

violence in its mouth
roosting a torrent
of red white and blue.

A row of freshly rained-on buses
are glinting like medals
on the chest of
an unwilling veteran.

The icy sidewalk
is a tray of knives
opening beneath me.

The thin grey line
of commuters at dusk
groping for tickets and passes,
like me,
dreaming of a utopia
of a two hour work day
endless sex and cinema
hand held devices for all
shelter from the Pompeii
of the day to day.

In the farmland
lowering itself below us
towards the Pacific
a silent suburbia
is drifting in invisible cliffs
between the car lights

staking its hope in the promise
of a larger loneliness
of concrete and glass.

The Misunderstanding

Perhaps
it was all a mistake

a slight
misunderstanding
between friends

we can all head home

be children again
forgetful, unknowing

the dead will all come back
and that together
we will remember nothing

history will unravel
its coiled whip

rivers will pack up
and head upstream

mountains relax
soften into friendly scree

volcanoes
will breathe in
instead of out

all that has happened
will not have been

all those that have suffered
will be freed

can put their feet up
take a smoke, drink tea.